CW00323925

Phillips
COLLECTORS GUIDES
TIN TOYS

Text ©	Nigel Mynheer
Illustration ©	Phillips Fine Art Auctioneers
Edited by	Linda Doeser
Designed by	Strange Design Associates

Copyright © Dunestyle Publishing Ltd and Boxtree Ltd, 1988

Boxtree Ltd.
36 Tavistock Street
London WC2 7PB

Conceived by Dunestyle Publishing Ltd.

ISBN 1 85283 231 2

Typesetting by Top Draw, London
Colour separation by J Film Process Co Ltd., Bangkok, Thailand
Printed in Italy by New Interlitho spa.

TIN TOYS

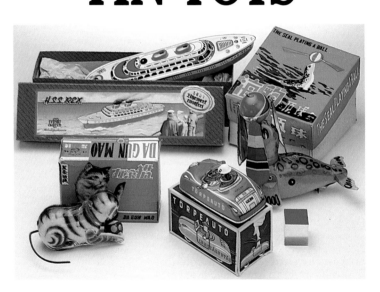

NIGEL MYNHEER

BOXTREE

Phillips, founded in 1796, has a reputation for specialisation. Its specialists handle fine art, antiques and collectors' items under more than 60 subject headings — a huge spectrum of art and artefacts that ranges from Old Masters and the finest antique furniture to cigarette cards and comparatively modern pop memorabilia. The auction group's Collectors' Centre, situated at Phillips West Two in Salem Road, Bayswater, London, is constantly recognising, defining and catering for new trends in collecting. It answers hundreds of queries a day from collectors, museums, dealers and the public at large. The shelves of its cataloguing halls are packed with a treasure-trove of objects, awaiting their turn to appear at auction. To varying extents, the scene there and in the main Mayfair salerooms (Phillips, 7 Blenheim Street, London W1Y 0AS; telephone 01-629 6602) is repeated at a score of Phillips branches elsewhere in Britain.

Contents

Introduction

The collecting of toys is a relatively recent phenomenon. It started seriously in the 1960s which saw the end of quality tin toy production with the advent of battery-operated space toys. Collectors and traders in the fine arts field tend to regard toys as mass-produced items and as bygones rather than works of art, but this is clearly not so as we see prices reaching thousands of pounds in the salerooms of international auction houses.

A person can begin collecting for several reasons. It may be that he sees a toy remembered from childhood which triggers off happy memories making him feel he would like to own it once again, or maybe he sees a toy that was beyond his reach as a child and the idea of owning it now is still as strong.

Two typically English early post-war transport toys with clockwork spring action by Wells. Both valued between £30-£50 ($50-$90) each.

The very nature and circumstances of a person's upbringing can influence the type of toy that he or she seeks to collect. Well-to-do families often spent large sums of money on quality German-made boats, cars and complex novelty toys, whereas poorer children could enjoy the charm of a penny toy or a yo-yo. The toys we had were not always of our own choosing but often given to us by parents and grandparents either at Christmas, on birthdays or perhaps on holiday. As collectors, however, we can seek out what appeals to us. Nevertheless, what appeals to one collector does not necessarily appeal to another as it is all very much a matter of personal taste. The value of the item is not the main issue here but rather its appeal and charm. Although

Left A German Carpet Toy Beetle, missing a considerable amount of paint due to the floor being its main area of play — probably trodden on rather often.

Below This postcard photograph taken in the immediate post-war period shows a limousine with electric lights and a rear view of a BETAL products Double Decker London Bus.

mass-produced it may be a masterpiece of design, lithography, handtooling or perhaps have some ingenious piece of mechanism and, for any one of these reasons, be considered a desirable toy to add to a collection. A tin toy, like any other man-made object, reflects an era or marks an occasion so the variety is unlimited in any field, with the exception of girls' toys, which were very seldom constructed of tin.

When starting a collection it is a good idea to pick a theme - either a period or a subject. Boat collections are far removed from robot collections in both period and the nature of the toy. Diecast model cars are the usual starting point until an appreciation of tin toys begins to take hold. Space for your collection may pose a problem, so after say, a year, when the collection becomes too large it can be made smaller by being more selective and selling the less desirable pieces in order to purchase one fine piece. In this way the value of the collection may be gradually improved.

The means by which toys become available are not as limited as it may seem. There is the attic or loft which has often yielded a neglected gift - banished by some spoilt child of a previous generation - which comes to light when the owners perhaps retire and dispose of the contents of their home by taking their wares to an auction house. Auctioneers are available to anyone who wants to sell, whether they represent a private or deceased's estate, an elderly person with no one to leave their possessions to or old shop stock. This makes the auction house a very good place to buy and auctioneers specializing in toys will also provide a catalogue. The

Right A German hand painted clockwork crawling beetle by Guntermann *c.* 1910. Hard to find in working order. £100($180).

Below A colourful clockwork motorcycle by Mettoy of England, sporting a negro clown rider. Early post-war, this example is not in excellent condition but will still command £50($90) upwards.

majority of items are of tin or zinc construction. Friends and colleagues are also a valuable source and are happy to lend a helping hand to a collector, often unearthing something of interest from their own family loft. Street markets are possibly the best hunting ground for bargains as they do not have expensive shop overheads and are therefore relatively inexpensive. Often their wares are obtained from local house clearances. These traders often frequent boot fairs held on most weekends throughout Europe.

By the nature of my work I find the auction houses in England and the USA the best providers of the largest variety of collectable toys at any one time. The newcomer can learn a lot by attending an auction and studying the catalogue available - this will describe the items on offer with an estimated price. Personal viewing is strongly recommended as condition is always based on opinion, so the true value is whatever the potential buyer considers it to be when he views. A collector sees a toy not only as an object of play but as a curiosity

and a potential investment, so competition can be fierce. I often hear someone saying 'I remember having one of those' and after attending the auction to buy the item that meant so much years ago, departs saying, 'The difference between a man and boy is the price of his toy'. It is sad to think that today's child is only momentarily thrilled with a computer game or a cassette, whereas our fathers' and grandfathers' generations were fortunate enough to have lived through the era of the printed tin toy.

A remote control, battery-operated, tin plate Ford Thunderbird by Yonezawa of Japan. Collectors of the model cars only pursue mint condition examples. Worth up to £150 ($270).

This book is intended as a guide for newcomers to toy collecting at all levels of income. Great pleasure can be derived from searching out examples, hunting for that elusive treasure to add to the collection and gaining the satisfaction from reaping rewarding profits as the collection improves. Toys have been around as long as mankind itself and there are many fields of juvenilia in which to venture but tin toys will always appeal to the more commercially-minded collector.

Chapter One

Aircraft

The BOAC Radiant at the top of the picture is by Schuco. The three Airliners by Marx and Linemar. All these aircraft are very similar in appearance and function. Still an exciting area to start collecting.

All the first aeronautical tin toys were directly inspired by the coming of man's achievement in flight itself with the production of the first toy aeroplanes in Germany around 1910 by Märklin and neighbouring factories. Airships also appeared at this time. The earlier examples were handpainted and later lithographed with identification numbers, but the manufacturers' names and trademarks were rarely stamped or printed on the craft. This now makes it difficult in most cases for collectors to identify the origin of such a toy.

Bi-planes appeared before monoplanes and are virtually extinct today as they were very expensive at the time of manufacture. Consequently, only the wealthy families could afford to buy them. These flimsy pieces of history scarcely appear on the open market as early toy collectors have acquired the only examples known and these are worth many thousands of pounds today.

The principal manufacturers of toy planes before the war were Märklin, Bing and Tipp Co., who produced a bi-plane bomber, lithographed in a striking finish in several different guises during the 1930s. This clockwork model actually carried and dropped diecast, moulded bombs housed under each wing in batches of three, and now commands a price of £200/$360 if in good condition. During this period many fighting craft evolved as a result of the feeling of air-fighting supremacy looming before the outbreak of war in 1939. Märklin produced a Junkers construction kit while Lehmann offered a similar but smaller model.

Aeroplanes are constructed of many components and the piecing together by soldering or

tabbing of the parts took considerable time. Consequently the price was high and has remained so for anyone wishing to acquire these models.

The motivation for aeronautical toys was rather limited because of the inability of the manufacturers to emulate flight. The early examples were push-along and trundle movement only, the floor or table top providing a suitable playing surface. The clockwork mechanism could provide a back or front propeller movement in conjunction with the two wheels or even drive an airship, suspended on a thread, causing it to career around in a circle at considerable speed, for up to a minute. Lehmann's Zeppelins, the EPL 1 and EPL 2 (the larger model), are good examples of this method of 'flight'.

A Lehmann Captive Balloon called Mars — a very rare toy. Nearing £1,000 ($1,800) in value.

Shuco produced a clockwork airliner which could set in operation four propellers, one by one, taxi along a distance and cut out the power to each motor singly before coming to a halt. These were exceptional toys at the time and now, with original box and instructions, fetch between £200-£250/$350-$450 at auction.

Helicopters and jets appeared in the 1950s and 1960s, made chiefly by Marx and Linemar. The larger planes of passenger airliner class were based loosely on Stratofortresses, Boeing Liners and USAF high performance jets. These were clockwork or battery-powered and packed into a box of very slim shape to accommodate the dismantled wings and fuselage.

The actions performed by post-war aircraft, whether friction or battery-operated, are very interesting and at the time of production, appealed greatly to the buying parent as well as the eager child.

The earlier models were always handpainted and hand-assembled, so they are easily distinguished from the later lithographed models which give detail to pilots, windows, bolts, registration numbers etc. These were all applied on a silver or

A clockwork high wing monoplane by Tipp Co. If complete with bombs can fetch up to £300 ($540).

camouflaged finish according to the duties of the aircraft on which the model was based. The Marx models were fairly plain, in silvered spray enamel finish, with their attractions displayed on the lid of the box. Almost all models from 1950-70 have a value of between £30-£60/$50-$90, low enough to be considered a good field for investment.

Aircraft toys are also desirable to a small group of collectors who do not see the item as a toy, but a representational model of the aeronautical world. Dinky toy

planes, die-cast in zinc and very small, seem vastly overpriced against the large tin-plate toy models. Although not rare, these items may be purchased at Aerojumbles and salerooms occasionally if, as can happen, a deserted shop stock comes up for auction and as the market is still being created rarity has not, as yet, been fully established.

There are several points to beware of when collecting aeroplanes. The main pitfall is the sticky lithography finish appearing on 1920s and 30s models from the German manufacturer, Tipp & Co., which often suffer badly from offprints from the newspaper wrappings. As this is not removable the value is reduced to less than half. Battery-operated models, if they have been neglected, suffer from corrosion of the battery box and should really be avoided as the

toy will be difficult to restore to working order.

Boxes for aeroplanes have seldom survived because of the jagged obtrusive shape of the toy being pushed and prodded back into its box, usually impatiently, thus destroying the carton fairly early in its use. Deteriorated boxes can give a clue to the manufacturer but not enhance the value of the toy. Price range £5-£5,000/$9-$9,000.

The Lehmann clockwork EPL.1 Zeppelin. Quite a few of these around still and if found in working order could fetch up to £150 ($270).

Chapter Two

Animals

A small collection of mainly German and Japanese animal toys ranging in value from £5 ($9) up to £100 ($180).

Animals appeal to children and adults worldwide, from pets, on an emotional and caring level, to a general concern with the protection of wildlife in all forms. In the toy world, animals of various species have been depicted in almost every conceivable pose and these toys engender widespread appreciation from collectors and animal lovers alike. The types of animal toys produced cover an extensive range from those performing natural actions through to personified animals capable of carrying out human activities such as knitting, rowing, reading, typing and playing musical instruments.

During the early post-war years, regulations were introduced regarding the manufacture of toys with sharp protruding edges. Consequently, animal toys, which had once been constructed of many tabbed pressings, became simpler and more rounded in finish.

From the turn of the century to the present day the countries producing animal toys have continued to be Germany, USA, Great Britain and France. The early examples were either push along or clockwork. The later toys produced in Japan and China are battery-operated and are sometimes remote-controlled.

Almost every toy factory included animal toys in their manufacturing as they knew the subject matter would be a good seller, appealing to both boys and girls, as well as to parents who would approve of a subject that could be easily recognized. These toys can be divided into types according to their roles. There are circus creatures, domestic animals and pets, wild beasts, zoo animals and character animals, such as those seen in cartoons, films and on television.

The most familiar of these are the Walt Disney characters which were used very effectively to market thousands of products.

The construction of animals is usually quite complicated, often incorporating many parts in order to emphasize the movements of legs, jaws and tails. The early German examples of dogs and insects can be found at reasonable prices, although the joints of working parts are often worn and scuffed due to their rubbing during motivation. The movements of these toys vary

from the simple pecking birds, ducks bobbing and quacking, to the more involved dogs performing tricks, cats playing ball, and chimpanzees and elephants performing circus tricks. Bears can be seen carrying out a wide variety of occupations,

Bears performing various human activities. Typical of the 1960s Japanese approach to battery operated novelty creatures.

such as a dentist, barber, writer, blacksmith, office clerk, photographer, boxer, gardener, marksman, cyclist, cook and fisherman, all basically the same size, but with slight modifications to the mechanism to suit the actions.

The Japanese manufactured battery-operated animal toys capable of singing, blowing bubbles, whistling, playing a tune

An unhappy looking clockwork Boxer Dog by Blomer and Schuler of Germany.

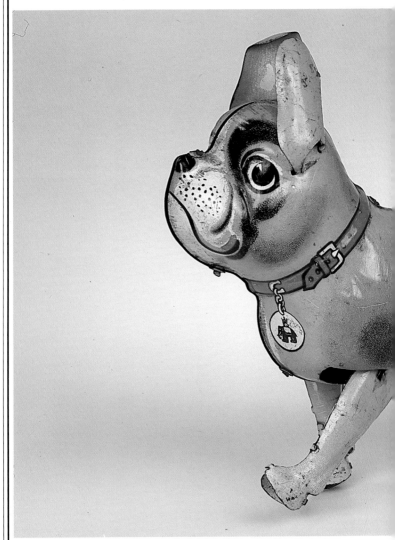

and even one breaking wind! These actions were all quite ingenious but, unfortunately, not made strong enough to last for long, so today it is difficult to find examples in a fully operative condition.

The rarity of some post-war toys makes them very expensive for collectors. A good example is 'Snappy the Happy Bubble-blowing Dragon' - a large toy

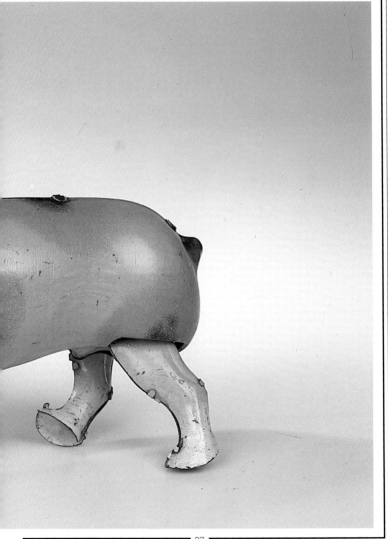

constructed of tin and plastic, and covered with plush. The battery-operated mechanism operates the articulated body, lights up the fins and motivates the animal with a swinging action until it stops and then blows bubbles. This ferocious, almost ridiculous, toy will fetch, with box, £1000/$1800 at auction.

American and Japanese products like these are not rare and may be found, with the original boxes for between £30-£50 ($50-$90).

Animal toys are generally easy to find as so many have been produced all over the world for the past eighty years. A visit to a boot fair or a flea market will always produce some examples at reasonable prices, but toy auctions will offer the largest selection, often displaying fifty or more examples at any one time.

As animals appeal to almost everybody, the collectors' range is very wide so it may be as well to specialize in a particular species, such as cats, bears or insects.

Boxes are not quite so important as in, say, boats or cars, but are certainly an added bonus. Prices range from £3/$5 up to £1000/$1800 but generally most examples are under £50/$90.

Chapter Three

Boats

Toy boats are the rarest of all old toys collected today and therefore command higher prices than any other field. They were fairly expensive to buy and were not such good sellers as trains or road vehicles. The child lucky enough to receive such a toy would have to live near a village pond, river or coast, otherwise his parents would not even consider purchasing a toy water-bound vessel.

The places where boats were played with were limited to the facilities nearby, as only the wealthy could travel in the early part of this century. In towns, the local parks had a yachting pond and in coastal districts there were boating pools and the sea. The countryside provided streams and rivers and smaller boats could be played with at home in the bath tub, wash basin or kitchen sink. However it is unlikely that it occurred to young folk to dry and oil the boat after playing with it and, therefore, thousands of examples became rusted and the mechanisms seized up. Consequently, when the following summer came round they were consigned to the dustbin.

Another reason contributing to their rarity and caused by their heavy construction, was their tendency to sink, often in unreachable places. Unless the onlooking parent was prepared to wade in and fish for it, the boat remained submerged.

The models produced came in different sizes from 3in (7.5cm) to over 3 ft (90 cm) in length, designed to suit the prospective purchaser's pocket; the grander versions were usually purchased by well-to-do families and today command thousands of pounds in the salerooms. It is only relatively wealthy collectors who can now

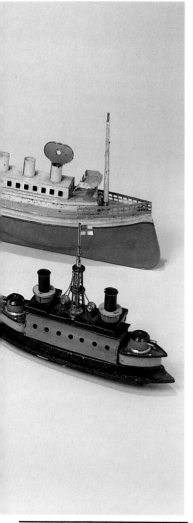

Back row — SS United States by Linemar, a J.E.P. (France) squat clockwork ocean liner. Several Hess and Carette carpet battle ships and in the foreground an In-dock floating crane boat. Worth between £30-£300 ($50-$500).

afford to buy them — particularly the examples equipped with gilt enamelled handrails, gorgons and composition figures taking refreshment on the upper decks. These early boats are not antiques of tomorrow but are already established as fine art objects.

Boats have always been expensive because of the many handmade components necessary, which themselves had to be put together by hand-soldering and tabbing. The general construction began as two pieces of pressed, convex-shaped, tin-plated steel shields held together by flanges or tabs and then soldered along the joints. This was then hand-painted in thick layers, especially along the underside of the hull to ensure the vessel was watertight.

The early toy boats were manufactured in the 1880s but the commercially successful models came between 1905 and 1915. These were highly detailed and very rarely carried a manufacturers' trade mark, so they are very difficult to attribute

The clockwork Plunging Pike by Bing. The majority of these toys were sunk in lake and river beds 75 years ago.

to a particular maker.

Toy boats have been manufactured in similar shapes and proportions to those of the real vessels throughout the past eighty years but modifications to details have been made in some cases. German manufacturers produced boats resembling ocean-going liners and war boats, loosely styled on famous craft so that proportions of the more exciting details were exaggerated to make the toy more attractive. Particular attention was paid to fanciful deck detail and included several flags made of linen and painted tinplate. Figures, either staff or passengers, were composition made (compressed baked flour and sawdust coated with plaster) or pressed lead enamelled in costume colours. These would be free standing or have a hole underneath them so that they could be placed on a spike sited on the upper deck.

The motivation of toy boats was generally a very strong clockwork spring key-wound motor placed at about mid-hull. This could last for a considerable amount of time — up to six hours — circling a pond many times and gradually becoming slower at the end of its journey. Spirit-fired boats needed more attention and seem to have been considered unsafe, so are very rare today. Because of the safety aspect and consequent lack of popularity, they were not produced in very large numbers.

Carpet toy boats and penny toys produced in the first quarter of the century have a certain charm due to the quality of lithography and survive well as they were never placed in water.

The types of boats produced covered every industrial example from ocean-going liners to torpedo boats, battleships, small launches, competition boats, submarines, river-trip boats and gun boats. Many of them carried a gorgon, figurehead, demon or a phoenix to act as a mask, giving protection to the crew against the devil of the deep blue sea.

The German manufacturers were leading pioneers of toy boat making, the prime makers being Märklin, Carette, Bing and

Schoenner. These were mainly clockwork or steam-powered and of high quality, produced for international markets with appropriate names and flags.

In England the models produced were relatively plain and not so detailed but were robust in construction. Sutcliffe was the main manufacturer, producing models from the mid-1930s until only several years ago. These models were long lasting but inexpensive, making them available to most people's pockets.

Meccano Ltd, of Liverpool provided a range of Hornby Speedboats, all driven by good clockwork motors which would run in excess of five minutes. They came in different sizes with two-tone colour schemes and sold extremely well. Exciting names were transfer-printed on the front of them, such as Racer, Vampire, Viking, Movette and Fregate, and they were finished in typical 1930s colours such as cream, white, green, red and blue. These models, in their original boxes, can be obtained at a price between £50-£150/$90-$270 depending on the size of the model and condition of the box.

Bowman models offered spirit-fired, rather undefined basic models of craft contained in a wooden box. Being well-made, they stood the test of time and can

be obtained for around £30/$50 upwards, again, depending on the size of craft.

Submarines are a good subject to study and collect. Although thousands were lost, there were very many examples produced so that it is possible today to see a wide variety of this type of craft at reasonable prices, from £30-£200/$50-$350. Sutcliffe's Unda-Wanda and Nautilus are examples very often seen and may be purchased for a modest £20/$32. A cork or rubber bung is used to block the key-wind hole to prevent water getting inside the vessel.

The German manufacturers, Bing of Nuremburg, made for the English market through Bassett-

Two German pre first world war clockwork boats by (left) Arnold valued at £250 ($450) and (right) Falk valued at £400 ($700). In a better condition they would command a higher price.

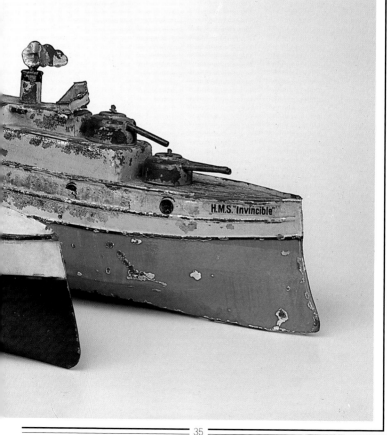

Lowke, a remarkable toy called the Plunging Pike. This was attractively enamelled in pink, grey and silver and, by means of the clockwork mechanism, submerged and re-emerged in the water using the submarine principle. Made in 1910, it is now worth £150/$270 — a price which does not reflect its aesthetic appeal and quality.

Packing for toy boats was usually of very poor quality cardboard, stapled together. It suffered from dampness as, more often than not, the young owner would put the boat back after use without first drying and oiling it. Bowman boats, however, were housed in a wooden carrying box-case and although the boats themselves were very plain and unexciting, this has enabled examples to survive to this day. The box also gives a guide to the country of origin and sometimes, the manufacturer, but does not enhance the value as much as, say, a Dinky toy with original box.

The pitfalls of investing or collecting tin toy boats mainly occur with repainted items. Early German boats are particularly easy to fake. Repainting can be hard to detect as the originals were hand-finished and had thick coats of paint applied to the lower hull regions. Restored pieces should be avoided unless the item is so rare that another is never likely to come on the market. Boats used in the sea are subject to varying degrees of salt-water corrosion and can never be renovated without destroying the original applied paintwork.

The rarity of boats adds to their desirability as far as collectors are concerned and because they are so popular boats will always be in

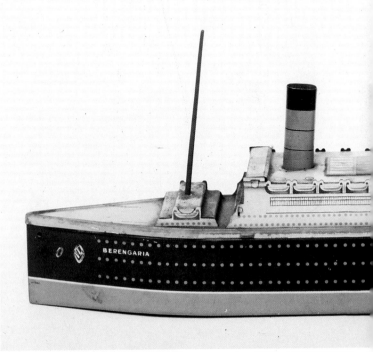

the highest price bracket.
However, lithographed penny toy
boats and simpler carpet toys of
the 1920s and 1930s can be
obtained for under £100/$180.

The main area to search is the
auction houses, where they are
usually sold in single lots, but
sometimes one can be lucky
enough to find an attractive
flywheel-driven boat included in
a lot of general novelty toys. The
coastal junk shops often produce
models of ships and occasionally a
tin boat will appear at an
acceptable price. However,
prices vary and it is very much up
to the individual to decide what he
is prepared to pay as there are no
guidelines laid down.
Commonsense should dictate
whether the price asked is
reasonable.

A tinplate biscuit tin by Crawfords. The upper
decks are removable to house the biscuits. This
1930s model appeals to toy collectors as it is really
a carpet toy.

Chapter Four

Boys and Girls

Tin toy collectors of today are made up of approximately 95 per cent males. This is probably because the operational nature of the object was originally directed at the son of the family rather than the daughter. The playthings for girls were generally more delicate in construction and less harmful. Made of bisque porcelain, fur or synthetic fabric and manufactured into teddy bears and dolls, they were more useful as a comforting companion than a noisy, articulate, tin novelty toy.

Toys shared by boys and girls were used out of doors. Sea-side buckets and spades were often lithographed with Disney characters, and in the garden children played with tambourines, pedal cars, scooters, swings and slides.

Construction kits for boys were very popular, comprising many pieces to be made into models of transportation and industrial vehicles relevant to each particular period. Parents were of the belief that a piece-together toy would improve their child's mind and aid his development, curiosity, determination and general capabilities — a forerunner of the so-called 'educational' toys of today.

In the 1960s, tin kit toys gave way to plastic kits of cars and aeroplanes and building bricks. The two dominant manufacturers of these items were Airfix which, instead of a nut and bolt assembly method, only required a touch of polystyrene cement, and, of course, Lego.

Meccano is the most famous form of builder-toy known to us all. In 1901, Frank Hornby of England took out a patent on a toy set entitled 'Mechanics Made Easy' which was the forerunner of the boxed Meccano sets, packaged

Typical boys' toys all manufactured in Germany. In the background two stationary spirit fired steam engines by Bing of Nuremberg and two operative accessories — the Blacksmith by Bing and the colour wheel by Märklin — 1910-1930

neatly with instructions on suggested models to be constructed. Many of these examples were mass-produced, so are readily found today at prices ranging from £30/$54 up to £300/$540 for a comprehensive wooden-boxed set. During the 1930s, Frank Hornby saw future development for specialist subject construction toys, appealing to all levels both from a simplistic and easily-affordable point of view, all aimed at the child with an inquisitive and slightly scientific mind.

Cars, always a favourite, were produced as constructor and non-constructor models, complete with instructions, nuts, bolts screwdriver and various components to alter the model from a sports car to a boat-tailed

racer. The parts were enamelled in bright primary reds, blues and greens, with cream-coloured additions and sporting a diecast driver with goggles who was included to add to the realism of the finished model. Meccano cars are now very desirable items among collectors but, because they were assembled and re-assembled several times, are rarely found with an unscratched finish. The mint examples range from £150/$270 for small versions up to £1000/$1800 for the larger, comprehensive kits.

Meccano aeroplanes, although not as successful as the exciting cars, came in a large box of many pieces with a choice of either a civil or military finish but, nevertheless, they now command between £100-£200/$180-$360 and

This Marklin Standard Petrol Tanker is a constructional toy produced in the late 1930s. Complete, in good condition it is worth £500-£800 ($900-$1,400).

are, of course, of great appeal to aircraft collectors.

Hornby boats came simply but colourfully boxed and are a typical English boy's toy, now realizing prices of between £60-£100/$108-$180.

In the USA, Gilbert offered marvellous constructor kits of locomotives contained in a wooden chest. Rarely found now, these are worth £100-£150/$108-$180.

German manufacturers distributed, through select English toy shops, many spirit-fired stationary steam engines

The girls' toys shown here are mainly dolls house furniture of German manufacture and by Rico of Spain. The girl with perambulator is by Goso, dating from the early post war years.

and trains. These were considered quite dangerous, which, indeed, they could be as pressure built up and, if mishandled, they would sometimes explode unexpectedly. 'Dribblers' and 'Piddlers' were so called because they deposited excess hot water puddles on the floor. As early examples of these are not rare, they can be acquired for £60-£100 /$148-180 each. These trains are comparatively simple in relation to the models sought by the perfectionists, but they have a very strong appeal to yesterday's child who was critically-minded enough not to be contented by the amusement or charm of a carpet toy.

In the 1930s Märklin offered fine constructional toys of vehicles which were produced up until 1953 and consisted of saloons, tankers and limousines, all sold with a separate constructional chassis. Now highly desirable, these toys can fetch between £400-£600/$720-$1080.

In France in the 1920s, JEP, (Jouets de Paris) manufactured quality motor cars for boys. Today these are valued at between

£500-£1000/$900-$1800. CIJ produced a P.2. Alfa Romeo in various colour schemes worth at present, up to £800/$1440 in its original box. Citroën models were also produced to a very high standard and are more true-to-life models than toys — these also fetch several hundreds of pounds.

Toy production for boys consisted of 'exciting' racing games, railway sets, military battlefields etc., whereas toys for girls had to possess qualities of a more appealing nature, be visually pretty and charming, easy to hold, thin in construction and non-mechanical. Apart from soft toys such as cuddly animals, they had Post Office sets with paper, envelopes and stamps, and sweet shops, manufactured by Pascalls, complete with miniature bottles and jars of sweets and scales to weigh them on. These were all highly decorative and, by their very

A Meccano Construction Car set from the late 1930s. Complete with all accessories in original box is worth £1,000 ($1,800).

nature, not very durable! There were very few tin toys made specifically with girls in mind. The main field incorporated doll's house related items and painted tinplate dolls' prams and beds. These are to be found at fairly inexpensive prices, probably due to their rather plain nature.

However, lithographed items, such as sewing machines, babies in perambulators or in high chairs, and based on a penny toy appearance are more desirable. In Japan during the early 1960s, factories produced battery-operated novelty toys constructed of tin and covered in fabric, depicting young girls performing daily duties such as pushing prams or as a seamstress, busy typist and busy secretary bashing out staggered rhythm on a tinplate typewriter. These toys are easily found, particularly at markets and car boot fairs at around £20/$36.

A Schuco Tele-steering car. Although fairly common in red is less frequently found in blue or green. Commanding a price of £60 ($100).

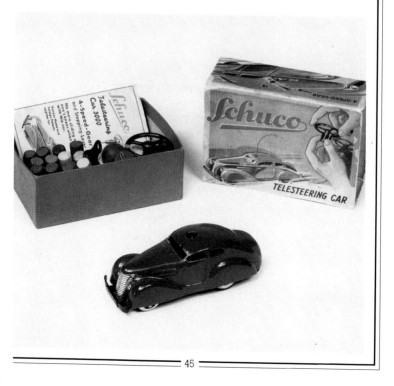

Chapter Five

Media Toys

Many media-influenced toys are based on a familiar character portraying a popular, recognizable image, hero or villain, which appeals to most children through comics, elevision and the film network.

The characters have a cartoon-like fictitious appearance, are usually brightly coloured and carry all the relevant accessories needed to convey the feeling of a larger-than-life image — the fastest, strongest, brainiest or

Made in USA and Japan. These toys are Disney characters, the train and lorry also appealing to transport toy enthusiasts.

whatever traits needed to make it the most appealing toy. The selling point of the product is usually concentrated on the familiarity of the character, rather than the often disappointing function of the toy itself.

A good example of a media toy is Batman, the law-abiding hero who survives endless perils to catch the crooks and put them safely behind bars. Only a few toys were produced, for example, a stylized Batmobile and a

battery-operated Batman. Even fewer were of tinplate construction. Most products were made of vinyl, including models of Robin and life-size playsuits. Diecast models were produced on a small scale by Corgi — the Batmobile with several working actions and, similarly, James Bond's Aston Martin car — both surviving in abundance today. By comparison, Japanese-manufactured tin-plate versions of both these cars are difficult to find and command prices of up to £80/$144 each.

Superman, another American comic and film hero from the 1930s, has only ever appeared as

Typical post war beach buckets made in England in the early post war years. These are hard to find in an uncorroded state. £5 ($9).

a lithographed image on tin toys such as aeroplanes and combat tanks. An actual model of Superman in tin was never produced. Tarzan and King Kong, the heroes of the jungle, were however, made into walking tin machines by Japanese manufacturers, but performance was limited to walking, turning of heads and the raising of arms.

Mickey Mouse is probably the most widely-exploited example of an international animal hero whose image has been depicted in almost every aspect of daily life. Manufactured into a soft, plastic or tin toy, Mickey Mouse appealed to boys and girls of all ages — and

to adults, too. He was so popular in America in the 1930s that at Christmas-time shops gave him a more prominent image than Santa Claus. Many products, however, were of poor quality, depicting Mickey, Minnie and friends Pluto and Donald Duck printed together around the toy. These characters have all been found performing many daily chores with astounding ability such as playing a xylophone, practising a magic trick, dancing, drumming, driving an engine or car, riding a motorcycle or even rowing a boat.

The main manufacturers in the earlier years — from the 1920s to the 1940s — were Distler from

Germany, Wells and Happyknak from England and Lionel and Marx in the USA. After World War II, a Japanese factory under the name of Linemar produced many toys which were well made, nicely coloured and presented in exciting packaging, today fetching £50-£200/$90-$360. Whenever these toys came on the market, irrespective of the period of manufacture, a Walt Disney Productions copyright sign appeared somewhere on the outer surface of the article. Objects found without this sign were not officially authorized and, although poorly pressed and printed, are very rare and expensive, appealing only to Disney Toy collectors.

Tipp and Company produced a clockwork, lithographed motorcycle with Mickey and Minnie Mouse as riders, aimed at the English market. Although a very attractive model, the lithography was very sticky causing paper and dirty fibres to adhere to the surface. Therefore 'clean' examples are very rare and attract a price tag of £1000/ $1800.

Several post-war toys, although mainly constructed of tinplate, have added components of plastic, vinyl, celluloid and felt fabric, but this does not detract

from their desirability. Girls'
Disney toys were of a practical
nature. Found nowadays in a
playworn state, these were picnic
and tea sets and crudely-printed
buckets and spades which soon
became rusty after a good day's
outing on the beach.

Many different heroes have
been sculpted into mechanical
toys. These include Popeye, Olive
Oyl, Wimpey and Brutus,
Dagwood and Blondie, Kayo and
Mullins, Charlie McCarthy, Topo
Gigio, the Flintstones, Donald
Duck, Pluto, Dennis the Menace,
Tarzan, Spiderman, The Pink
Panther and many more, all
mass-produced for as long as they

Mickey the Musician on the left is a smaller version
of a similar toy while Pluto is the larger version of a
smaller counterpart. All items at around £100
($180).

A seaside boat by Happynak Toys of England.

remained popular in the eyes of the media.

As collectors concentrate on one character, they will notice how the materials used in production alter with the years — tinplate models being overtaken with wood, bisque porcelain, soft filled toys, celluloid and printed ephemera. This means that it will be difficult for the general toy collector to purchase tin toys in the media category.

The interest in collecting media toys is very wide-ranging, extending to the USA where most of the collectors of Disney characters live. In England, collectors are content to collect TV adventure characters from the 1960s, such as Dr Who or The Saint, and 'Children's Hour' characters such as a Noddy and Big-Ears, Dougall and other familiar friends. However, although many media toys are produced they are usually short-lived, being well played with and often misused by their young owners; batteries are run down, detachable pieces removed never to be replaced, and general neglect creeps in once the novelty interest wears off and the latest character takes pride of place.

Certain toys collected today lose more than half of their value if, for example, Bubble-blowing Popeye is rusty inside, or Mickey the Magician has lost the chick under his hat. These relatively minor defects can reduce the price from £150/$270 to under £50/$90.

Chapter Six

Novelty Toys

Novelty toys first appeared in the eighteenth century, developing further in the nineteenth century with automata, through to the early 1900s when toys were mass produced. The International Exhibition of 1851 saw the introduction of German tin toys to England. China, Japan and France also produced toys for export which were sold to retailers in boxes of a dozen.

Around the turn of the century, in France, Ferdinand Martin manufactured hand-enamelled toys featuring people from ordinary walks of life including barbers, sailors, blacksmiths and even beer keg porters and street violinists. Many of these toys carry no maker's mark but are easily recognizable and give the enthusiast an extra interest to research his new find. These toys sold very well in France, which is still the best hunting ground for them today. In Germany, however, competition between the factories was very fierce. This may well have led to the high standard of quality which was reached very quickly, particularly in the first three decades of this century, bringing success to the larger companies. Part of their success, however, was due to the government support they received, as these companies exported to as many countries as their representatives could reach.

In 1944, because of the war and also because a large number of Jewish companies were involved in the production of toys, toy manufacture was stopped. After the war these companies had great difficulty in starting up again, family contact and business associates having lost touch with each other. This left the way open for Japan to take the upper hand in toy production. German toys, however, were far superior in

A selection of 1960s toys from Mark (USA). Clockwork 'Nutty mad Indian' £80 ($140); a battery operated 'Yeti' and a 'Walking Tiger' £100 ($180) each. Although not entirely constructed from tin — these toys incorporate rubber, vinyl and fur fabric as well — they provide a good area for collecting, if in good working order.

A German US zone early post war clockwork toy of two boxers. It is worth between £60-£80 ($110-$140).

ONE GERMANY

many ways, with the subjects portrayed ranging from domestic activities to sporting games such as billiards, snooker, skiing, gliding, shooting, dancing and sweeping.

Penny Toys are an exclusive category and appeal to a certain type of collector interested in small toys, usually miniaturized versions of vehicles or topics of purely novelty appearance. The mechanism was kept very simple. They were either wound by a handle or pushed along on the wheels fixed to the base platform, sometimes aided by a central inertia flywheel.

The manufacturers in this field were all German; Fisher, Kellerman, Meier and Distler produced thousands of examples between 1905 and the outbreak of World War II. These would have been exported by the dozen to England and sold in street markets in London by board vendors in Hoxton, Petticoat Lane, Ludgate and The Friars, costing one penny each. Construction was simple, consisting of pressed thin tin pieces tabbed together on to a wheeled undercarriage. The subjects were chiefly day to day amusements, in particular animals, circus entertainers, babies, balloon travel, zeppelins, cars, lorries and trains — in fact, all objects depicting the changing social activities of the time.

For the collector, the desirability of these toys lies not so much in their rarity but in their aesthetic appearance, although condition is very important as many of these frail toys are subject to rust because of their thin, tinny, construction. Their collectability is unlimited in that many slight variances in form and colour occurred within examples of the

Made by Marx (USA) between the late 1930s and the early 1960s, all these toys display clever actions using clockwork and battery operated motivation, as well as having a pleasing design appeal. £50-£100 ($90-$180) each.

same product, thus the price range is £15-£100/$27-$360.

The first step in construction was to put the proposed design on paper and make detailed drawings of the mechanism to be fitted. After this a wooden template was carved, to be used for constructing the mould. Several moulds would be needed to make all the individual components which would later be tabbed by hand. The mock-up or prototype was usually far removed from the finished product. The tinsmith would cut and press the required pieces after the hand-enamelling process or application of lithography. After assembly, the item would be varnished and baked. Early toys were held

together by soldered joints but most examples have slots into which tabs were inserted and then folded over to hold the parts together.

Mechanisms for novelty toys varied considerably, from free-wheeling, clockwork, friction, candle-heat or elastic bands to electricity and battery power. At the beginning of the century the process of offset litho on to the tin plate from rubber rolls saved the necessity for hand-spraying and hand-painting and produced nicely printed, clear and precise images on the relevant surfaces of the toy. Hand-painted toys are very expensive involving more skilled

One of Germany's earlier fly-wheel driven toys by Lehmann, 'Kadi', the two China men carrying a tea-chest. This toy is worth in excess of £500 ($900).

people for assembly and finishing which required lining, stencilling and the application of faces or lettering.

Louis Marx of the USA manufactured thousands of cheap but amusing clockwork novelty toys, brightly coloured and presented in eye-catching packaging, mainly working on themes of well-known characters that would be very easily identifiable. These toys were sold in great numbers, not only in toy shops and department stores but by direct-mailing lists. As so many have survived today, they can be purchased for a reasonable sum — in fact many post-war examples are under-rated. £20-£150/$36-$270.

Ethnic groups are also portrayed as toys, mostly from the 1920s to the 1950s and, by the use of clever clockwork motors, appear tap-danciing, playing a banjo or boxing to name but a few actions. Negro-faced tin money boxes, although of poor quality, can be very decorative.

Soon after the end of World War II, the Japanese started to produce toys made from discarded cylindrical drink and food cans, remoulded and cut to shape. Due to low production costs and very cheap labour, output was high and the market boomed as the toys were inexpensive. They were brightly coloured and although not always a totally original idea, had a certain slick appeal. If carefully dismantled however, their humble origins could be clearly seen. The packaging for these toys was also bright and appealing but, sadly, was not made of very good quality cardboard and boxes found today are invariably rather faded or tatty.

Many of the examples produced contain a clockwork

mechanism but during the late 1950s and 1960s, batteries were more commonly used to enable the toys to perform two or more functions including walking, talking, flashing lights, blowing bubbles and even smoking. Sometimes they were operated by remote control. There were quite a number of Scotsmen produced, depicted in traditional Scottish dress and constructed mainly of tin but covered in felt fabric with rubber heads and plastic accessories. A good example of the genre is Charlie Weaver, the bartender, who shakes, pours and downs his drink, sways from side to side and goes bright red in the face. This popular, though not expensive toy can be purchased today in the auction room for as little as £30 ($43), or £45 ($81) with original box, but check the battery box for corrosion or the toy will not function.

There are two Japanese toys which, although rather strange, are very much sought after by collectors. One is known as the Spooky Kooky Whistling Tree. this is battery-operated and to a child, very frightening in appearance and action. It can fetch today between £300-£500/ $540-$900. The high price may well be because not many of them were bought at the time of marketing, as parents did not consider them suitable for children and liable to give them nightmares! The other is the Haunted House which is quite a large toy and has many novelty actions including a howling wind noise, skeletons, ghosts and cats popping up at random out of chimneys and windows. It was all operated by a single battery motor and was great fun. This toy, which was well printed and attractive, can be bought with the

Four Lehmann clockwork novelty toys. 'Ski Rolf' £700 ($1,260); 'Paddy and the pig' £1,000 ($1,800); 'Oh My!' £200 ($360); and 'The new century cycle' £500 ($900).

original box for around £300/$540, although I feel sure that this will appreciate quite quickly in the near future.

In England, novelty toys were not manufactured in any quantity until after the 1920s and, more particularly, after World War II. Before that time supplies were readily available from the French and German markets. The most prominent English manufacturers were Wells, Mettoy (of German origin) and Chad Valley, which also produced a large assortment of indoor methodical toys and games and took over Burnett which made interesting spring action vehicles. Sutcliffe Pressings has been making boats since the 1920s but only a few have novelty interest and are usually basic in design. Sometimes a Noddy figure would be added as a driver in order to sell the product.

As there are numerous manufacturers and novelty subjects available, it may be easier to begin collecting a theme rather than trying to collect a particular make of toy. Because companies sprang up and disappeared quickly it is often the distributor's name which appears on the box, for example Cragstan and S.S.S.INT., but they did not make the toy and this can make identification very tiresome.

Below A French clockwork clochard, dressed in fabric. When wound he stumbles and staggers along. This toy dates from the turn of the century £150 ($270). A German tinplate money bank. £100 ($180).

Press the lever lightly,
Watch my tongue appear,
Save a penny nightly,
Make your fortune here.
MADE IN GERMANY

Below The 'Whistling Spooky Kooky Tree' by
Marx, more of a science fiction oddity than a space
toy

With post-war novelty toys the
age is not important — it is the
degree of desirability which
seems to be the main factor,
whether the field chosen is space,
animals, vehicles or 'spooky' toys.
Condition, on the other hand, is
all-important. If an item is in mint
condition with original box and is
worth, say, £100/$180, the same
toy, slightly incomplete,
scratched, not functioning
properly and minus its box, could
drop in value to less than £20/$36.
So points to watch out for and
avoid are rust, rotting nylon fabric,
perished rubber components,
overwound clockwork motors
and corroded battery packs.

If a comic character is depicted
on a toy it may well appeal to a
collector in another field and,
therefore, the price will be
higher. Patience will, however,
reward those who search, which
is after all where the fun lies, and
the same toy may well turn up
elsewhere at half the price.

Availability is enormous as
novelty toys were sold worldwide,
and sometimes old shop stocks
appear on the market. If a
particular toy should appear
which, although not necessarily
rare, several collectors wish to
own, the demand may inflate the
price to an unreal level, especially
in a toy auction where all
interested parties attend. The
auction houses actually set a
market price, so it is well worth
making sure results sheets are
obtained for future reference for
pricing a particular buy.

Chapter Seven

Railways

The Royal Scot Train Set by Hornby from the 1930's. Unusual to find in this excellent condition. £500-£700 ($900-$1,250) with box.

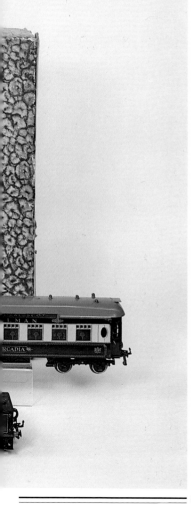

Railways are essentially a practical toy for overgrown boys, so collectors tend to be railway enthusiasts concerned with the intricacies of the lines and system and the authenticity of the models. In other words they are 'buffs' rather than collectors simply appreciating the items for their individual charm or for their lithography or toy appeal.

Trains were in strong competition with boats and planes as successful sellers and as all boys were interested in turn-of-the-century toys, the size of the object became all-important to the parent buyer. Sets varied in size to cater for the modest buyer and the wealthy consumer. At the lower end of the scale, small penny toys of the push-along type were available; they were quite basic but had clever detailed lithography applied to the outside of the structured body.

Bing of Germany produced a tabletop railway of narrow gauge (almost 00) motivated by a clockwork or electric motor which, as a complete boxed set, can be acquired for as little as £80-£150/$140-$270. Carpet toys of thin tin body were also miniature models, loosely based on a complete passenger train with a simple push-along, flywheel-driven, inertia mechanism.

When toy railways evolved, a model train was an exaggerated toy rather than a representational engine, and the details such as the chimney, domes, lamps and stokers' footplates etc., were enlarged to emphasize its similarity to the original. The first toy trains were manufactured in Germany by Bing and Märklin in the 1890s, motivated by clockwork or spirit-fired steam. The outer shells were mostly hand-enamelled with the lithographed pieces appearing later, at the turn

Left A clockwork version of the Royal Scot by Bassett-Lowke — probably more accurate and true to scale than its Hornby counterpart. Worth £500-£600 ($900-$1,050).

Below Two German lineside accessories by Bing — a Destination Indicator and a Candle-lit Signal Box.

of the century. This company, along with another by the name of Carette, produced fine train sets of very good quality, which were purchased by wealthy families for their offspring as educational toys as well as playthings.

The 0 gauge system was the most popular gauge for railways, later progressing to gauge 1 and up to 7¼ in (18 cm) for use in the garden, a practice in which the wealthy members of society, with time and money on their hands, were able to indulge.

In 1900, at a trade fair in Paris, an Englishman, W. Bassett-Lowke, met the German manufacturer, S. Bing. They decided to combine forces in order to promote the toy railway market in England and offer sets at affordable prices. This they did and became an extremely successful partnership, producing some very fine train sets.

The Germans continued to dominate the market devising gauges of rails in sizes 0, 1, 2, 3 and 4. Their output was enormous. Germany had a huge workforce and the rates of pay were low. Therefore, it was able to export to countries such as the USA and Great Britain in large numbers and at reasonable prices. Bing and Bassett-Lowke made charming lithographically-printed, boxed sets, with key and instructions, which, when set out on the kitchen floor or empty tabletop gave pleasure to many a young lad.

In England, the leading manufacturer was Bassett-Lowke, making fine models of steam, electric and clockwork trains, in several gauges, but they were very expensive. The company of Bowman made spirit-fired steam locomotives. Although usually plain, they were very well made and many survive today. These can be purchased for £50-£100/

Wagons of O gauge and OO gauge, Petrol wagons and others. Any carrying company advertisements are the most desirable. £5-£300 ($9-$550).

$90-$180.

Then, in the 1920s, Meccano Ltd. of Liverpool produced the famous Hornby '0' system, which was designed to suit everybody's pocket, starting with the simple boxed sets and working up to the more sophisticated models, which later included three-rail electrical trains made throughout the 1930s. These sets were produced in large quantities, available over most of Europe and, because they were well made and boxed solidly, they have survived well. If the collector is patient enough, he will be able to collect a whole range, whether it be by decade, livery, goods and passengers sets or just line-side accessories. Prices today range from £20/$36 for an 0-4-0 'M' series locomotive to £1100/$1980 for a 'Princess Elizabeth' and tender, with original box, which just two years ago, was only £450/$180. Examples of the Royal Scot and the Flying Scotsman are rapidly climbing from £120-£200/$216-$360.

Other English manufacturers were Wells and Chad Valley who manufactured cheaper range train sets with simple, but pleasant, lithography, not only on the rolling stock but cleverly applied to the lineside accessories, especially tunnels

and stations with a typical countryside feeling.

Ever-Ready produced a crude but very individual Red London Transport Underground set which would probably only have appealed to London boys. It is now fetching up to £80/$180.

The American company, Lionel of New York, offered robust 0 gauge Electric Flyer type trains which are most sought after in the USA but in England they can be collected at very reasonable prices as they do not have very great appeal to the English collector.

00 gauge sets were popular in

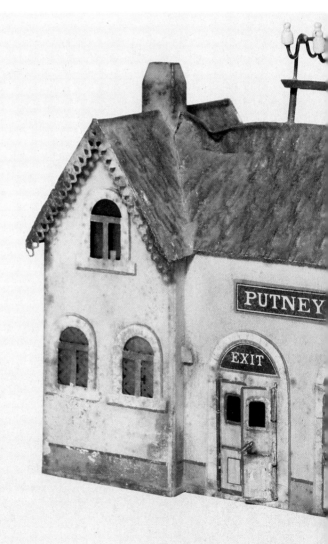

the early post-war years and because they did not require a lot of room, a comprehensive set was not too expensive. Trix of Germany exported good electric sets, but only the rolling stock was of tinplate construction, the locomotives were made of diecast zinc. In England, the Hornby-

A Candle-lit German Station made for the London market.

Dublo was of similar construction, with tinplate track and wagons, some representing companies of oil and petrol distributors or brick and coal companies. These can be picked up today for as little as £5-£10/$9-$18 each.

Lineside accessories of all gauges could form an interesting collection of their own, the goods yards, stations, luggage trunks and even newspaper kiosks, all possess degrees of charm and quality of printing depicting an era of railway travel of this century. The Germans, as usual, were pioneers in this field, creating, in miniature, every image which could be found alongside the real railway.

As all train sets were manufactured in vast quantities, there is a good survival rate and they have a great appeal to collectors today, so any objects which were expensive at the time of manufacture are the most sought after. Therefore, a high price not only reflects rarity but also the level of desirability. A good example is the Hornby Eton locomotive and tender which, because it is very attractive, has increased in value within two years from £200/£300 to £1,000 ($360/$540 to $1,800) — quite an inflation!

Boxes for trains are an added bonus, but as they are usually plain and not illustrated, they are not as important as, say, novelty toy packaging. The presence of a key however is a useful addition.

The collector's range is unlimited as train sets can be picked up at auctions, swap-meets, railway collectors' clubs and at boot fairs. Prices are

Typical lineside buildings of O gauge proportions. All English except the chimneyed station at the top by Bing.

extremely varied, but most examples are probably underpriced at the moment and provide a very good ground for investment if pieces are chosen carefully rather than bought at random.

A Der Adler train set by Marklin of Germany made in 1936 as a limited edition to commemorate 100 years of the train's history..

Chapter Eight

Road Transport

A GAMA (George Adam Mangold) 1950s cadillac from West Germany. A fine example of a post war boy's toy, appealing very much to American collectors. It can fetch up to £500 ($900) with the original box.

Man-made objects have been depicted in the toy world. They quite often mark an event or the introduction of an invention. This is particularly the case in the transport world where, since the turn of the century, a toy car may appear in the shops at the same time as the real vehicle.

The motor car itself was on the road in 1893 and by 1903, several toy examples were available. Smaller models, like penny toys, lost detail of mechanism but were always set on wheels to provide some simple movement. At first, very few motor cars were made as the car itself was not a popular invention from the public's point of view. Consequently, very few early examples survive today and those that do are considered very fine 'works of art'. In auction, these can fetch many thousands of pounds — often more than the original motor car itself!

Models varied considerably in price, depending on whether they were hand-enamelled or printed. The lithographed versions were usually smaller and less expensive. The addition of such details as lamps, glass windows, luggage trunks, composition drivers, footmen, chauffeurs, and sometimes passengers, added to the charm and reality of the model and also to the price. This was especially so with the top of the range models, which had rubber tyres and working electric lamps.

After World War I, the manufacture of toys altered in that lithographed details were printed on tin sheets which were cut out and tabbed together. This, in turn, made them lighter and cheaper to produce; with mass-production came greater availability. Drivers and passengers became pressed tin and printed rather than hand-painted figures.

Rossignol of France produced attractive, good quality, examples of light pressings in its racing cars and vans. Delivery vans and buses made in Germany were directed at the English market, carrying advertisements for home products such as food, holidays, or games and toys manufactured by the same factory. English delivery vans and lorries tended to advertise at every opportunity and examples of these products included Carrs Biscuits, MacFarland and Lang, Crawfords, International Stores, Gray-Dunn, Mackintosh's, Chad Valley Toys and Betal Products. Some of these toys actually contained the product itself.

All toy makers produced road vehicles at some point during their years of manufacture. The main examples from Germany were Bing, Märklin, BUB, Guntherman, Fisher, Distler, Hess, Tipp Co., Lehmann, Meier

A group of post war cars mainly made in England. £5-100 ($9-180) each

A clockwork omnibus by Bing made in 1911. In nearly mint condition, this toy realised £8,500 ($15,300) in 1987.

and Eberl. In America, Marx and Wyandotte offered typical American long-bodied saloon cars with powerful clockwork spring motors. In England from 1930 onwards, there was Mettoy, Wells, Chad Valley and Meccano Ltd. The post-war Japanese makers such as Linemar, Marusan, Yonezawa, Nomura, Tomy, Asahi, Daiya and Ichiko, usually distributed by Cragstan, offered very good representational models of classic 1950s and 1960s American saloons — a good field for today's collectors in the £50-£300/$90-$540 price range.

Exciting racing and record cars appeared in the 1930s, heavy in construction, housing powerful clockwork motors and exceeding 1 ft (30 cm) in length. Each box depicted white flashes of rushing wind to portray the speed of the vehicle, with the driver only visible as a small white crash helmet in a large streamlined machine. The makers of these

A CIJ (France) clockwork P2 Alfa Romeo racing car which was available in various colour schemes. This example recently fetched £780 ($1,400) at auction.

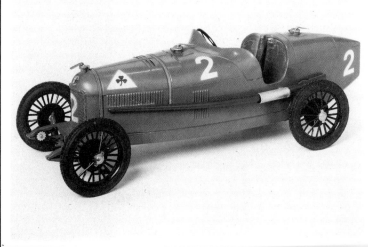

cars were Guntherman and Kingsbury and they were modelled on the Sunbeam, Silver Bullet, Golden Arrow and Bluebird. Smaller, more basic versions of these models were produced in England by Chad Valley. Survivors of this era are usually either playworn or rusty, having been used out of doors, but in mint condition with original box, they can fetch in excess of £200/$360.

Tipp Co., in Germany, made quality clockwork cars with exaggerated long bonnets and plenty of seats. these had novelty extras such as opening doors, battery operated front and rear lights and a chauffeur. The body work was lithographed with elegant lines in complementary two-tone colour schemes of red with grey, brown with beige and green with cream. Three years ago an example would cost £200/$360, but they are now commanding nearer £1,000/$1,800 and are likely to exceed this

A German clockwork Gordon Bennet racer by Guntherman of Germany, *circa* 1904. An example in good condition could fetch £4,000 ($7,200) at auction.

In England, Lines Brothers offered pre war and post war Triang minic vehicles. They have recently tripled in value despite the fact that it is rare to find one that works.

figure in years to come.

The English counterparts produced by Wells, Chad Valley and Mettoy were squarer in design and flimsier, with sharp protruding edges at all corners of the structure making them generally inferior and thereby reflecting the price of £30-£100/ $54-$180 for a mint example. Post-war figures of drivers have determined faces, as if always in a hurry, and they are dressed in caps and uniforms associated with delivery boys.

GAMA (George Adam Mangold) produced probably the best example of a post-war toy car — the 1950s Cadillac, available in various colours with a million-dollar grin, radiator grille. Displaying all the good qualities of a fine toy, this car is now worth £400-£500/$720-$900.

Toy motor cycles have become a collectors' field in themselves in the last two years, so prices can be high when a rarity appears at an auction. In Germany the pioneers of these toys were Schuco, Tipp and Arnold, and in England, novelty bikes were made by Mettoy also of German origin.

A colourful collection of clockwork motor cyclists, all of German manufacture, including Tipp and Schuco examples.

Right The Chad Valley delivery van lithographed with many products available from the company e on the roof. £200 ($360).

The many pieces required to assemble these toys were lithographed with engine details, racing numbers and riders in striking protective overalls. A good clockwork motor sent the bike whizzing around in circles. Arnolds MAC 700 model allows the rider to dismount and remount the cycle whilst it is in motion. This ingenious toy is worth £500/$900 in working order, whilst the clever examples by Schuco which were built to last are fairly common and can be purchased for £50-£200/$90-$360.

Toy cars of high quality are being produced by the Spanish company PAYA, made from the original pressing moulds used in the 1920s. They can be purchased new today and, although costly due to hand-production, provide an interesting collecting area for tomorrow's antiques.

The survival rate of toy road vehicles is high, as there were more of them produced than any other type of toy. Another reason is that they are more likely to be cared for because they are often used just as models and decorative items in a boy's bedroom rather than thrown away when broken, which is the fate of most toys.

The collector's range is very popular in this field as all grown-up boys associate themselves with cars from the era of their childhood, whether it be father's or the next-door neighbour's car, or possibly the milkman's float, coal lorry, or the bus caught to school. The field is very varied, as are the prices which start at £5 and can go up to £25,000/$9-$45,000.

Above: A Tipp Co (Germany) lithographed clockwork limousine with electric lights. A desirable toy having risen in value from £200 ($360) to £1,000 ($1,800) in the past two years.

Below A Marx clockwork Doughboy tank, commonly found at £30-50 ($54-90)

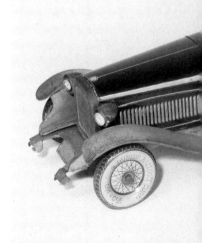

Chapter Nine

Space Toys

Two 1960s toys from Japan. The Yoshiyo robot is worth £100 ($180).

Space toys are usually fun toys and have a distinctive collectors' zone of their own. Those interested usually follow a theme, sometimes from a television influence or from a certain period of interplanetary travel.

The design of spacecraft was developed from early post-war aircraft based on futuristic assumptions. This has now evolved to a slimmer and more vertical craft and, with the advent of the jet turbine, propeller engines are no longer part of the design.

As a result of man's achievement in beginning to conquer space in these post-war years, several feature films and comics have developed a graphic art style for the machines, aliens and transport forms which could possibly materialize as objects of interplanetary exploration. All of this has helped to create a market for the manufacture of space toys.

The fact that Sputnik hit international news in the 1960s stimulated toy manufacturers, particularly in Japan, with space-orientated images familiar to many people. Several manufacturers had produced earlier clockwork versions, but in America and Japan, battery-operated models of exploratory machines, moon walkers and games began to appear. Most of these were functional and somewhat exaggerated rather than depicting an actual craft or vehicle that has marked history.

Several robots command very high prices at auction, starting at £30/$50 and soaring to £1100/$2000. As these are relatively recent collectors' items, the reason must surely be that examples unpopular at the time of release in the shops were quickly withdrawn from the production line and so now are very rare.

Charm or appeal, does not necessarily make a robot toy desirable as unattractive models, such as Robbie and Mr Atomic, change hands in excess of £1000/$1800 each. Collectors of such items appear to need to acquire every known example, so a rarity appearing on the market can fetch an absurd price whether it be a cereal packet gift, tin lunchbox, film poster or any related ephemera which comes under this heading. This is particularly so in Japan and the USA, whereas the market in

Several clockwork and battery operated robots, satellite and astronaut toys. All with their original boxes — an essential part for the collector.

England is only just slowly catching on.

Space toys can be found at auctions but prices are high as many Americans subscribe to the catalogue — particularly at Phillips which has been selling robots for the past two years. Bargains are only to be found by local advertising or regularly attending jumble sales, markets and boot fairs.

The London Toy Museum in Paddington holds a representative collection dating from the early post-war years to current times, but most examples have now found homes in private collections. Prices range from £5-£1,200/$9-$2,500.

Robots provide the main interest in this section and are an excellent area for study and investment, particularly in England, as the American and Japanese markets are fairly well-established. Early space toys, all clockwork, are constructed from tabbed-together lithographed tinplate with added plastic accessories. The later examples, usually battery-

operated, finally gave way to the diecast and rubber space monsters currently available. Today's versions of these toys are of a durable nature, with very clean lines and a cold, clinical appearance. Their movements are usually of a domestic nature, such as sweeping or cooking. Some, however, can do somersaults, play music and the more sophisticated even have voices which give out commands or offer some verbal communication. Prices for these vary from £6 up to £100/$10-$180 and they could be collectable in years to come.

In comparison, the tin robots of the 1950s and 1960s have a warm, friendly appeal in spite of their menacing appearance with guns and antennae to search out and exterminate their enemies. These early examples are scientifically interesting in form, the bodies being very cubist in design, with square heads, oblong truncated bodies and rectangular limbs. When wound up, the movements were very slow but sturdy. The outside casings were lithographed with simple spherical dials on the chests, surrounded by bolts and rivets. These mechanical toys would be tabbed together in several parts in a rather flimsy fashion, but this added charm to the intended 'tinny' image. These early creatures were most likely created from the crude illustrations portrayed in the pulp science fiction publications that were popular in the 1930s, and the American 'B' movies surely had an influence on the image of space aliens unknown to all of us.

Robots are capable of performing many remote-controlled actions. These include lights, rotating hands, firing machine guns, raising of arms,

walking, talking and even smoking. The leading manufacturers of these novelty space toys were Nomura, Yoshiya, Yonezawa, Horikawa, Masudaya, ALPS, Taiyo, Aoshin and Daiya. The exporters and distributors whose names are found on the packaging are SSS and Cragstan, both operating from Japan. In the USA, Louis Marx and Linemar monopolized the robot market with toys that varied from space tanks, capsules, rockets, astronauts, Martians and moon patrol vehicles to satellite stations.

The boxes in which these toys were marketed were constructed of very poor quality thin cardboard, stapled at the ends, but graphically designed in a dynamic way to portray the toy inside as a powerful, menacing intruder, displaying many actions. The enclosed toy however, was very far removed from this somewhat exaggerated image.

Above right These four 1960s battery operated robots are similar in construction but perform different actions. Left to Right: Robot 8; Attacking Martian; Television Space Man; Smoking Robot. Prices range, with boxes, from £150-£1,100 ($90-$2,000)

Right Two versions of the 'Planet Robot' by Horikawa of Japan. The clockwork version has a different box.

Chapter Ten

Packaging

The box in which a toy was presented for sale probably comprised half the selling point of the object and talented, professional graphic illustrators have been employed to design the packaging for most products throughout toy packaging history. These clever cartons were designed to appeal as much to the parent making the purchase as to the child concerned and, just as important, to the shop retailer, who would have to purchase a large bulk order to obtain a reasonable discount and thereby make a worthwhile income. However, it can be clearly seen from surviving illustrated boxes that the toy pictured in action with a realistic background differs quite considerably from the product inside and is very misleading in terms of what movements or actions the toy is capable of performing.

Unfortunately, the thin cardboard used in toy packaging was not intended to have a long life span and, not surprisingly, very few boxes survive today. Those which do were probably unwanted gifts, or perhaps the child was simply uninterested in the toy, so it was put aside.

Occasionally, a shop would come upon hard times and the toy stock would remain untouched until a new proprietor moved in and changed the business, at which point unwanted goods would often be put into auction, surprising collectors with an unlimited choice of the same items. Consequently, the price would be slightly lower than normal because of availability. Such an event provides a good opportunity to obtain some mint and boxed examples for the collection.

Some boxes have a function to complement the toy, such as a

Catalogues of a company's products can themselves form an interesting collection and are very important in helping to date and identify certain variations and models as well as showing the original prices.

backdrop, a garage or a target board, and are usually found in a very playworn and tired state. A great deal of consideration and thought was given to the design of these cartons, not only the surface picture, but the way in which the casing could be folded and tabbed to add to the environment and play value of the toy. Some boxes have had a variety of images printed on their lids, while still containing the same product, presumably with the intention of attracting more sales. Good examples of these changes are the early Lehmann novelty toys and Japanese battery operated robots which also changed their name from 'Robot-Man' to 'Moon-Man' to 'Radical-Man'. Certain boxes carried a polythene or transparent celluloid front; this was not usually used for tin toys but for toys of diecast zinc in which the visible vehicle or item was the main selling point.

The noticeable difference between pre-war and post-war boxes is that 1950s and 1960s Japanese products, distributed by SSS and Cragstan are illustrated on top and on all four sides, whereas earlier cartons were often only plain brown cardboard with a gummed stick-on label in monochrome, showing the toy in an action-packed illustration.

Some of the most charming packaging is that of the pre-war Hornby 0 gauge train-sets, depicting steam passenger trains in a typical English landscape, while USA manufacturers, Marx, have three tone line drawings of typical American industrial scenes.

Boxes are as much of a find sometimes and as exciting as the toy itself. Apart from adding 20 per cent to the value, they are a very good guide to the manufacturer or country of origin as the trademark appears on the box, not the toy.

Although seldom seen, manufacturers' catalogues are interesting and essential for identification, as well as giving the original prices. Those found generally have a retailer's stamp and were not available to the

general public. Prices range from £3-£100/$5-$180 which is surely not expensive for supplying so much information. Reprints of the catalogues of the German factories and the Gamages range are available, but are not valuable as they are not original.

All clockwork tinplate toys were sold with a key, the finer models having a stylish key sometimes bearing the manufacturers' name. Japanese keys tend to be thin and plain, whereas early German boats sometimes have a fixed key in the form of a small cloud of smoke. The type of key is not really an important factor, so long as it winds the toy and serves its purpose successfully, as a standard gauge will accommodate many toys from different countries.

Left Examples of post war packaging, the images graphically presented in bright colours to make the toy look very attractive. These boxes have survived well and will add 15/20% to the value of the toy.

Below An early box lid from a German Train Set, probably by Bing, illustrating many of the toys which were available.

Acknowledgements

The author wishes to thank
Christopher Halton and Douglas
Howden for their photographic skills
and patience, Jacqueline Barber for
photographic archive material and
special thanks to Margaret Barber for
all her assistance in assembling the
final script.

A selection of Keys for pre and post war clockwork
toys. The small, rather plain, examples at the
bottom of the picture are from Japanese toys.

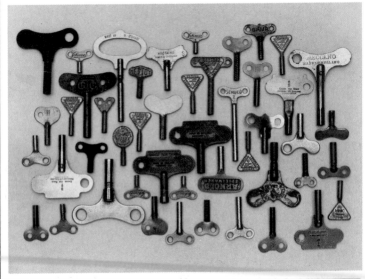